A Turning Point in Higher Education

A Turning Point
in Higher Education

The Inaugural Address

of Charles William Eliot

as President of Harvard

College, October 19, 1869

With an Introduction by Nathan M. Pusey

Harvard University Press

Cambridge, Massachusetts 1969

© Copyright 1969 by the President and Fellows of Harvard College
All rights reserved
Distributed in Great Britain by Oxford University Press, London
Library of Congress Catalog Card Number 79-91628
SBN 674-91339-6
The photograph of Charles William Eliot in 1870 is courtesy of
the Harvard University Archives
Printed in the United States of America

Introduction by Nathan M. Pusey

On the raw and cloudy afternoon of Tuesday, October 19, 1869, Charles William Eliot formally took office as President of Harvard University. Something of the breathlessness and excitement of the occasion, and the feeling that it presaged the dawn of a new day, is contained in the record of witnesses. Theodore Lyman wrote:

> At 2.30 we formed and a little after 3, we were all seated, [in the First Parish Church then used by the University for its largest ceremonies] I, of course, among the Overseers; . . . The galleries were quite filled with ladies and the body held many distinguished people . . . The Governor [William Claflin] came out, as of old, with the escort of Lancers; and sat on the platform looking much interested. After Music and Prayer, Gov. Clifford — as President of the Overseers — addressed the President elect and handed him the seal, keys, and charter. I was surprised at the weakness of this paper (which he read) — It was in form of a lecture to the new Chief, and took great pains to enter a caveat against certain kinds of "science." Clifford grows old . . . Charles replied in a dozen emphatic words — (which woefully brought out the length of the previous speech) — and took the old chair midst great applause . . . Then, after a chorus, "Domine fac salvum Præsidem nostrum," the President advanced to a little reading stand and delivered his Address. I had looked for a very good, sound discourse, but this went far beyond all I had expected! It was in style clear, elegant, and terse; in matter comprehensive and critical. His views of what a University should be were beyond praise. Such a volley never was fired before in these old walls; and yet there was nothing "radical" about it. They were one and all content with this address — most were even enthusiastic! [1]

If at the time of its delivery Mr. Eliot's words seemed of remarkable importance, viewed retrospectively from this point in time his address was a momentous event in the history of American higher education. Majestic in tone and style, striking in metaphor, abounding in new insights, it

1. Henry James, *Charles W. Eliot, President of Harvard University 1869-1909* (Boston and New York: Houghton Mifflin Company, 1930), I, 226–228.

v

gave focus to the aspirations and preachments of a small group of restless and impatient college leaders in the post-bellum United States and heralded the beginning of a fresh approach to university studies.

Until then the American accomplishment in higher education had been pitifully slight. There had been a few brave attempts here and there by those who recognized its deficiencies to break through the stifling influence of the old curriculum of standard courses and rote learning, including attempts at Harvard from the days of George Ticknor. Yet even of Harvard, as Henry James has written, "the best that could be said . . . appeared to be that she was leading a column of laggards." [2]

Some forty years after Ticknor's premature effort at reform the times were propitious. In the busy years following the Civil War and reconstruction the nation as a whole was girding itself for new ventures. There was a continent to be settled, and a feeling of progress and inevitable achievement in the air. Something of this spirit had been caught by the Reverend Thomas Hill, President Eliot's immediate predecessor, in his final report after six years in the presidency of Harvard College. For all the criticism that has been leveled against Hill for his ineffectuality and lack of personal quality and leadership, this sweet and gentle man set forth firmly and strongly the case for a new kind of education and for the creation in America of a university worthy of the name:

If our University desires to maintain her position as one of the first institutions in the country, she must not be content with hearing *memoriter* recitations from a text-book in the undergraduate course, but must devise stimulants to original investigation, research, and experiment; creating a class of students whose ambition it shall be to advance science, rather than to receive knowledge and diffuse it . . .

A University, richly endowed with chairs of pure science . . . does

2. *Ibid.*, p. 208.

not exist in the country; it is a national want; and its need is testified by the multitudes of young men from America who are found in the German universities.

The easiest place in which to found a university of a high order is Cambridge. The addition of two hundred and fifty thousand dollars a year to our income, or the direct gift of four millions to our capital, would do more toward making Harvard College able to supply the national need than the gift of eight or ten millions to any other college, unless it be Yale . . . it is a national need that we should have a true University; the best hope of creating one is at Cambridge, and it can be done here at much less pecuniary expense than anywhere else . . . It is more important to the country to have a university professor giving the highest instruction and highest known science to two or three young men of ability and industry, than that classes of a thousand should be studying in ordinary text-books.[3]

Many concerned for Harvard apparently shared this view, and now a leader was at hand. President Eliot was profoundly aware of the role he must fill in reforming American higher education, in building strongly on the foundation of discontent which many, including his predecessor, felt concerning the worth of college studies and the inadequate support which they were receiving from the graduates and friends of American institutions of higher learning.

Mr. Eliot was graduated from Harvard College in 1853 and in the subsequent decade served as tutor, assistant professor of mathematics, and assistant professor of chemistry. When he missed his chance for Harvard's Rumford Professorship, he left Cambridge for two years of travel and study abroad and then accepted a professorship of chemistry at Massachusetts Institute of Technology. It was from the Institute that he was called back to Harvard.

Mr. Eliot came to his task in a period of deep personal tragedy. His election to the presidency by the Corporation

3. Thomas Hill, "Forty-second Annual Report of the President of Harvard College to the Overseers, Exhibiting the State of the Institution for the Academical Year 1867–68" (Cambridge, Mass.: Welch, Bigelow, and Company, Printers to the University, 1868), pp. 11, 18–19.

occurred on March twelfth, the day before the death of his beloved wife, who lived long enough to learn the great news, but it was not until May nineteenth, after a series of delays because of opposition in the Board of Overseers, that Mr. Eliot's election was confirmed.

The college of Mr. Eliot's undergraduate years had consisted of only 383 students and a teaching staff of forty-four, including the President. The institution which he took over in 1869 had a faculty of sixty-three and 1,050 students. By the end of his forty-year tenure Harvard had grown to a community of seven hundred teachers and 3,900 students.

Mr. Eliot was barely thirty-five when he assumed the presidency. Despite his earlier success in college administration and his knowledge of faculty polity, he was beseiged by doubt as to his fitness for the presidency. He was deeply conscious of the need to say something of real substance which would serve as a rallying point for the educational forces seeking cogent expression. It seems likely that he sought the views of many in preparing his address. He consulted Professor George J. Brush of Yale as to his "responsibility in stating the case between the old and the new education (to use a phrase of which I am getting heartily sick)." He asked Brush to meet him and suggested the neutral ground of Springfield, where Brush and Daniel Coit Gilman (later Eliot's long-time friend, and President of Johns Hopkins) could discuss "how the École Centrale education and the ordinary American college education are to be made to understand each other. Also how scientific education in this country is to be improved. Also what higher opportunities of culture are needed in the country than colleges and scientific schools now offer. Also how the calling of professor is to be made more attractive to ambitious young men." [4]

On the day of its delivery, it was not so much the original-

4. James, *Charles W. Eliot*, I, 224–225.

ity of his inaugural address as the way he spoke it, the force of his personality, the trend of his argument, and the aptness of his speech to the times which impressed his hearers and the larger public. It was as if the machinery were ready to work and all sensed that in Mr. Eliot a man had appeared with the capacity to seize control and to advance the cause with conviction and vigor. His tone was confident, strong, determined. He stated his case with clarity. His message carried a sense of urgency. His definition of the role of the university is still a ringing exposition of the importance of learning in its broadest sense. "The only conceivable aim of a college government in our day is to broaden, deepen, and invigorate . . . all branches of learning." He argued for the reformation of the teaching of traditional subjects, and a fundamental rebuilding of the whole of education from the earliest grades. He argued for the humanizing and rationalizing of university studies, for extending them to include all languages, including "the mother tongue," for the natural and physical sciences, for mathematics, for mental, moral, and political philosophy, and for "living history." He spoke eloquently against dogmatism in teaching. He urged the development of impartial standards for admission and then, in a long central section, justified the system of elective studies which had been gradually developing at Harvard and which he was to bring to fulfillment.

It is remarkable that so much of Mr. Eliot's address has enduring value for us today. I have been especially impressed with how well his perceptive and illuminating comments about the roles of the Governing Boards have stood the test of time. For those brooding about the governance of universities there is obviously matter of importance here. But there are a few points of difference. Making allowance for the temper of his era and the values of the community he was to serve, it is not surprising to find him allowing only a slight place for women in his University. He paid tribute to the new experiment of opening extension courses to competent women, seeing in this departure a means of fulfilling women's desire for "liberal culture in studies which have no direct professional value, to be sure, but which enrich and enlarge both intellect and character," thus contributing to "the intellectual emancipation of women." But at the same time he made it quite clear women were not to be admitted into the College, "nor into any school whose discipline requires residence near the school." There now appears a degree of quaintness in this attitude.

Similarly, his remarks concerning university science indicate no deep understanding of how far scientific research might be carried nor the responsibility of universities for entering this line of endeavor. For him teaching was of prime importance. He also shared fully the belief of his time in the self-improvement of the people and the ultimate perfectibility of human nature. He saw no limits to the ultimate fulfillment of the desire of democracy for knowledge and competence.

But in championing democracy Mr. Eliot also gave frank expression to the need for an elite. He called for an aristocracy, not of family, class, or inherited position, but of the able and educated who, if they would only aim high enough, would liberate ambition and inspire in the people a high level of responsibility, initiative, and public concern. The purpose of education, he held, was to prepare men for the service of democracy. Like others of his generation he believed above all in enterprise and education, a high level of general education for all and a superior — and later specialized — education to prepare the informed experts needed as an indispensable ingredient in a democratic society. The true end of education, he said, is "effective power in action." He assumed such power would serve the common good.

Finally, Mr. Eliot pleaded for a spirit of maturity in college life. He effectively used terms like manliness and purity, which are not current parlance but still say something of qualities which surely mark the university at its best. One can imagine the impatience with which men of Mr. Eliot's nature would view the current university scene. He expected students would always be polite and would always eagerly pursue their studies. He spoke of "scholarly tastes and habits," "eager friendships and quick hatreds," "keen debates" and "frank discussions" as safeguards against "sloth, vulgarity and depravity," and urged his young hearers, in the part of his address spoken directly to them, not to be ashamed of showing admiration for a teacher. Rather they were urged to "cherish the natural sentiment of personal devotion to the teacher who calls out your better powers." Later he spoke in noble terms of "an aristocracy to which the sons of Harvard have belonged and, let us hope, will ever aspire to belong — the aristocracy which excels in manly sports, carries off the honors and prizes of the learned professions, and bears itself with distinction in all fields of intellectual labor and combat; the aristocracy which in peace stands firmest for the public honor and renown, and in war rides first into the murderous thickets." For Mr. Eliot Harvard will make two primary contributions to the country, "a rich return of learning, poetry and piety" and a fostering of "the sense of public duty — that great value which makes republics possible."

The grandeur of Mr. Eliot's words and concepts leaves us today deeply conscious of our failure to live up to all the goals he set for this University. But most of Harvard's failures have been human ones, and if we have learned anything in the past hundred years, it is to be suspicious in a way less palatable to Mr. Eliot's generation of the universal goodness of mankind. We are more conscious of man's possibility of redemption than of his perfectibility. Yet Mr. Eliot speaks of university work in a way we can understand, and the sound of his inspiring phrases, although intended for another generation, comes down to us with a brightness and clarity which can be an inspiration to our time.

If the true worth of a speech is to be measured by its constructive effect, President Eliot's inaugural is surely one of the very great addresses in the literature of American higher education. It is a privilege for a successor to introduce it, and a great satisfaction to know that his words will once more be generally available through this volume of the Harvard University Press.

A Turning Point in Higher Education

The endless controversies whether language, philosophy, mathematics, or science supply the best mental training, whether general education should be chiefly literary or chiefly scientific, have no practical lesson for us to-day. This University recognizes no real antagonism between literature and science, and consents to no such narrow alternatives as mathematics or classics, science or metaphysics. We would have them all, and at their best. To observe keenly, to reason soundly, and to imagine vividly are operations as essential as that of clear and forcible expression; and to develop one of these faculties, it is not necessary to repress and dwarf the others. A University is not closely concerned with the applications of knowledge, until its general education branches into professional. Poetry and philosophy and science do indeed conspire to promote the material welfare of mankind; but science no more than poetry finds its best warrant in its utility. Truth and right are above utility in all realms of thought and action.

It were a bitter mockery to suggest that any subject whatever should be taught less than it now is in American colleges. The only conceivable aim of a college government in our day is to broaden, deepen, and invigorate American teaching in all branches of learning. It will be generations before the best of American institutions of education will get growth enough to bear pruning. The descendants of the Pilgrim Fathers are still very thankful for the parched corn of learning.

Recent discussions have added pitifully little to the world's stock of wisdom about the staple of education. Who blows to-day such a ringing trumpet-call to the study of language as Luther blew? Hardly a significant word has been added in two centuries to Milton's description of the unprofitable way to study languages. Would any young American learn how to profit by travel, that foolish beginning but excellent sequel to education, he can find no apter advice than Bacon's. The practice of England and America is literally centuries behind the precept of the best thinkers upon education. A striking illustration may be found in the prevailing neglect of the systematic study of the English language. How lamentably true to-day are these words of Locke: "If any one among us have a facility or purity more than ordinary in his mother-tongue, it is owing to chance, or his genius, or any thing rather than to his education or any care of his teacher."

The best result of the discussion which has raged so long about the relative educational value of the main branches of learning is the conviction that there is room for them all in a sound scheme, provided that right methods of teaching be employed. It is not because of the limitation of their faculties that boys of eighteen come to college, having mastered nothing but a few score pages of Latin and Greek, and the bare elements of mathematics. Not nature, but an unintelligent system of instruction from the primary school through the college, is responsible for the fact that many college graduates have so inadequate a conception of what is meant by scientific observation, reasoning and proof. It is possible for the young to get actual experience of all the principal methods of thought. There is a method of thought in language, and a method in mathematics, and another of natural and physical science, and another of faith. With wise direction, even a child would drink at all these springs. The actual problem to be solved is not what to teach, but how to teach. The revolutions accomplished in other fields of labor have a lesson for teachers. New England could not cut her hay with scythes, nor the West her wheat with sickles. When millions are to be fed where formerly there were but scores, the single fish-line must be replaced by seines and trawls, the human shoulders by steam-elevators, and the woodenaxled ox-cart on a corduroy road by the smooth-running freight train. In education, there is a great hungry multitude to be fed. The great well at Orvieto, up whose spiral paths files of donkeys painfully brought the sweet water in kegs, was an admirable construction in its day; but now we tap Fresh Pond in our chambers. The Orvieto well might remind some persons of educational methods not yet extinct. With good methods, we may confidently hope to give young men of twenty or twenty-five an accurate general knowledge of all the main subjects of human interest, beside a minute and thorough knowledge of the one subject which each may select as his principal occupation in life. To think this impossible is to despair of mankind; for unless a general acquaintance with many branches of knowledge, good as far as it goes, be attainable by great numbers of men, there can be no such thing as an intelligent public opinion; and in the modern world the intelligence of public opinion is the one condition of social progress.

What has been said of needed reformation in methods of teaching the subjects which have already been nominally admitted to the American curriculum applies not only to the University, but to the preparatory schools of every grade down to the primary. The American college is obliged to supplement the American school. Whatever elementary instruction the schools fail to give, the college must supply. The improvement of the schools has of late years permitted the college to advance the grade of its teaching, and adapt the methods of its later years to men instead of boys. This improvement of the college reacts upon the schools to their advantage; and this action and reaction will be continuous. A university is not built in the air, but on social and literary foundations which preceding generations have bequeathed. If the whole structure needs rebuilding, it must be rebuilt from the foundation. Hence, sudden reconstruction is impossible in our high places of education. Such inducements as the College can offer for enriching and enlarging the course of study pursued in preparatory schools, the Faculty has recently decided to give. The requirements in Latin and Greek grammar are to be set at a thorough knowledge of forms and general principles; the lists of classical authors accepted as equivalents for the regular standards are to be enlarged; an acquaintance with physical geography is to be required; the study of elementary mechanics is to be recommended, and prizes are to be offered for reading aloud, and for the critical analysis of passages from English authors. At the same time the University will take to heart the counsel which it gives to others.

In every department of learning, the University would search out by trial and reflection the best methods of instruction. The University believes in the thorough study of language. It contends for all languages, — Oriental, Greek, Latin, Romance, German, and especially for the mother-tongue; seeing in them all one institution, one history, one means of discipline, one department of learning. In teaching languages, it is for this American generation to invent, or to accept from abroad, better tools than the old; to devise or to transplant from Europe, prompter and more comprehensive methods than the prevailing, and to command more intelligent labor, in order to gather rapidly and surely the best fruit of that culture and have time for other harvests.

The University recognizes the natural and physical sciences as indispensable branches of education, and has long acted upon this opinion; but it would have science taught in a rational way, objects and instruments in hand, — not from books merely, not through the memory chiefly, but by the seeing eye and the informing fingers. Some of the scientific scoffers at gerund grinding and nonsense verses might well look at home; the prevailing methods of teaching science, the world over, are, on the whole, less intelligent than the methods of teaching language. The University would have scientific studies in school and college and professional school develop and discipline those powers of the mind by which science has been created and is daily nourished, — the powers of observation, the inductive faculty, the sober imagination, the sincere and proportionate judgment. A student in the elements gets no such training by studying even a good text-book, though he really master it, nor yet by sitting at the feet of the most admirable lecturer.

If there be any subject which seems fixed and settled in its educational aspects, it is the mathematics; yet there is no department of the University which has been, during the last fifteen years, in such a state of vigorous experiment upon methods and appliances of teaching as the mathematical department. It would be well if the primary schools had as much faith in the possibility of improving their way of teaching multiplication.

The important place which history, and mental, moral, and political philosophy, should hold in any broad scheme of education is recognized of all; but none know so well how crude are the prevailing methods of teaching these subjects as those who teach them best. They cannot be taught from books alone; but must be vivified and illustrated by teachers of active, comprehensive, and judicial mind. To learn by rote a list of dates is not to study history. Mr. Emerson says that history is biography. In a deep sense this is true. Certainly, the best way to impart the facts of history to the young is through the quick interest they take in the lives of the men and women who fill great historical scenes or epitomize epochs. From the centres so established, their interest may be spread over great areas. For the young especially, it is better to enter with intense sympathy into the great moments of history, than to stretch a thin attention through its weary centuries.

Philosophical subjects should never be taught with authority. They are not established sciences; they are full of disputed matters, and open questions, and bottomless speculations. It is not the function of the teacher to settle philosophical and political controversies for the pupil, or even to recommend to him any one set of opinions as better than another. Exposition, not imposition, of opinions is the professor's part. The student should be made acquainted with all sides of these controversies, with the salient points of each system; he should be shown what is still in force of institutions or philosophies mainly outgrown, and what is new in those now in vogue. The very word education is a standing protest against dogmatic teaching. The notion that education consists in the authoritative inculcation of what the teacher deems true may be logical and appropriate in a convent, or a seminary for priests, but it is intolerable in universities and public schools, from primary to professional. The worthy fruit of academic culture is an open mind, trained to careful thinking, instructed in the methods of philosophic investigation, acquainted in a general way with the accumulated thought of past generations, and penetrated with humility. It is thus that the University in our day serves Christ and the Church.

The increasing weight, range, and thoroughness of the examination for admission to college may strike some observers with dismay. The increase of real requisitions is hardly perceptible from year to year; but, on looking back ten or twenty years, the changes are marked, and all in one direction. The dignity and importance of this examination has been steadily rising, and this rise measures the improvement of the preparatory schools. When the gradual improvement of American schools has lifted them to a level with the German gymnasia, we may expect to see the American college bearing a nearer resemblance to the German Faculties of Philosophy than it now does. The actual admission examination may best be compared with the first examination of the University of France. This examination, which comes at the end of a French boy's school-life, is for the degree of Bachelor of Arts or of Sciences. The degree is given to young men who come fresh from school, and have never been under University teachers: a large part of the recipients never enter the University. The young men who come to our examination for admission to College are older than the average of French Bachelors of Arts. The examination tests not only the capacity of the candidates, but also the quality of their school instruction; it is a great event in their lives, though not, as in France, marked by any degree. The examination is conducted by college professors and tutors who have never had any relations whatever with those examined. It would be a great gain, if all subsequent college examinations could be as impartially conducted by competent examiners brought from without the college and paid for their services. When the teacher examines his class, there is no effective examination of the teacher. If the examinations for the scientific, theological, medical, and dental degrees were conducted by independent boards of examiners, appointed by professional bodies of dignity and influence, the significance of these degrees would be greatly enhanced. The same might be said of the degree of Bachelor of Laws, were it not that this degree is, at present, earned by attendance alone, and not by attendance and examination. The American practice of allowing the teaching body to examine for degrees has been partly dictated by the scarcity of men outside the Faculties who are at once thoroughly acquainted with the subjects of examination, and sufficiently versed in teaching to know what may fairly be expected both of students and instructors. This difficulty could now be overcome. The chief reason, however, for the existence of this practice is that the Faculties were the only bodies that could confer degrees intelligently, when degrees were obtained by passing through a prescribed course of study without serious checks, and completing a certain term of residence without disgrace. The change in the manner of earning the University degrees ought, by right, to have brought into being an examining body distinct from the teaching body. So far as the college proper is concerned, the Board of Overseers have, during the past year, taken a step which tends in this direction.

The rigorous examination for admission has one good effect throughout the college course; it prevents a waste of instruction upon incompetent persons. A school with a low standard for admission and a high standard of graduation, like West Point, is obliged to dismiss a large proportion of its students by the way. Hence much individual distress, and a great waste of resources, both public and private. But, on the other hand, it must not be supposed that every student who enters Harvard College necessarily graduates. Strict annual examinations are to be passed. More than a fourth of those who enter the College fail to take their degree.

Only a few years ago, all students who graduated at this College passed through one uniform curriculum. Every man studied the same subjects in the same proportions, without regard to his natural bent or preference. The individual student had no choice either of subjects or teachers. This system is still the prevailing system among American colleges, and finds vigorous defenders. It has the merit of simplicity. So had the school methods of our grandfathers, — one primer, one catechism, one rod for all children. On the whole, a single common course of studies, tolerably well selected to meet the average needs, seems to most Americans a very proper and natural thing, even for grown men.

As a people, we do not apply to mental activities the principle of division of labor; and we have but a halting faith in special training for high professional employments. The vulgar conceit that a Yankee can turn his hand to any thing we insensibly carry into high places, where it is preposterous and criminal. We are accustomed to seeing men leap from farm or shop to court-room or pulpit, and we half believe that common men can safely use the seven-league boots of genius. What amount of knowledge and experience do we habitually demand of our law-givers? What special training do we ordinarily think necessary for our diplomatists? In great emergencies, indeed, the nation has known where to turn. Only after years of the bitterest experience did we come to believe the professional training of a soldier to be of value in war. This lack of faith in the prophecy of a natural bent, and in the value of a discipline concentrated upon a single object, amounts to a national danger.

In education, the individual traits of different minds have not been sufficiently attended to. Through all the period of boyhood the school-studies should be representative; all the main fields of knowledge should be entered upon. But the young man of nineteen or twenty ought to know what he likes best and is most fit for. If his previous training has been sufficiently wide, he will know by that time whether he is most apt at language or philosophy or natural science or mathematics. If he feels no loves, he will at least have his hates. At that age the teacher may wisely abandon the school-dame's practice of giving a copy of nothing but zeros to the child who alleges that he cannot make that figure. When the revelation of his own peculiar taste and capacity comes to a young man, let him reverently give it welcome, thank

God, and take courage. Thereafter, he knows his way to happy, enthusiastic work, and, God willing, to usefulness and success. The civilization of a people may be inferred from the variety of its tools. There are thousands of years between the stone hatchet and the machine-shop. As tools multiply, each is more ingeniously adapted to its own exclusive purpose. So with the men that make the State. For the individual, concentration, and the highest development of his own peculiar faculty, is the only prudence. But for the State, it is variety, not uniformity, of intellectual product, which is needful.

These principles are the justification of the system of elective studies which has been gradually developed in this College during the past twenty years. At present, the Freshman year is the only one in which there is a fixed course prescribed for all. In the other three years, more than half the time allotted to study is filled with subjects chosen by each student from lists which comprise six studies in the Sophomore year, nine in the Junior year, and eleven in the Senior year. The range of elective studies is large, though there are some striking deficiencies. The liberty of choice of subject is wide, but yet has very rigid limits. There is a certain framework which must be filled; and about half the material of the filling is prescribed. The choice offered to the student does not lie between liberal studies and professional or utilitarian studies. All the studies which are open to him are liberal and disciplinary, not narrow or special. Under this system the College does not demand, it is true, one invariable set of studies of every candidate for the first degree in Arts; but its requisitions for this degree are nevertheless high and inflexible, being nothing less than four years devoted to liberal culture.

It has been alleged that the elective system must weaken the bond which unites members of the same class. This is true; but in view of another much more efficient cause of the diminution of class intimacy, the point is not very significant. The increased size of the college classes inevitably works a great change in this respect. One hundred and fifty young men cannot be so intimate with each other as fifty used to be. This increase is progressive. Taken in connection with the rising average age of the students, it would compel the adoption of methods of instruction different from the old, if there were no better motive for such change. The elective system fosters scholarship, because it gives free play to natural preferences and inborn aptitudes, makes possible enthusiasm for a chosen work, relieves the professor and the ardent disciple of the presence of a body of students who are compelled to an unwelcome task, and enlarges instruction by substituting many and various lessons given to small, lively classes, for a few lessons many times repeated to different sections of a numerous class. The College therefore proposes to persevere in its efforts to establish, improve, and extend the elective system. Its administrative difficulties, which seem formidable at first, vanish before a brief experience.

There has been much discussion about the comparative merits of lectures and recitations. Both are useful, — lectures for inspiration, guidance, and the comprehensive methodizing, which only one who has a view of the whole field can rightly contrive; recitations, for securing and testifying a thorough mastery on the part of the pupil of the treatise or author in hand, for conversational comment and amplification, for emulation and competition. Recitations alone readily degenerate into dusty repetitions, and lectures alone are too often a useless expenditure of force. The lecturer pumps laboriously into sieves. The water may be wholesome, but it runs through. A mind must work to grow. Just as far, however, as the student can be relied on to master and appreciate

11

his author without the aid of frequent questioning and repetitions, so far is it possible to dispense with recitations. Accordingly, in the later college years there is a decided tendency to diminish the number of recitations, the faithfulness of the student being tested by periodical examinations. This tendency is in a right direction, if prudently controlled.

The discussion about lectures and recitations has brought out some strong opinions about text-books and their use. Impatience with text-books and manuals is very natural both in teachers and taught. These books are indeed, for the most part, very imperfect, and stand in constant need of correction by the well-informed teacher. Stereotyping, in its present undeveloped condition, is in part to blame for their most exasperating defects. To make the metal plates keep pace with the progress of learning is costly. The manifest deficiencies of text-books must not, however, drive us into a too sweeping condemnation of their use. It is a rare teacher who is superior to all manuals in his subject. Scientific manuals are, as a rule, much worse than those upon language, literature, or philosophy; yet the main improvement in medical education in this country during the last twenty years has been the addition of systematic recitations from text-books to the lectures which were formerly the principal means of theoretical instruction. The training of a medical student, inadequate as it is, offers the best example we have of the methods and fruits of an education mainly scientific. The transformation which the average student of a good medical school undergoes in three years is strong testimony to the efficiency of the training he receives.

There are certain common misapprehensions about colleges in general, and this College in particular, to which I wish to devote a few moments' attention. And, first, in spite of the familiar picture of the moral dangers which environ the student, there is no place so safe as a good college during the critical passage from boyhood to manhood. The security of the college commonwealth is largely due to its exuberant activity. Its public opinion, though easily led astray, is still high in the main. Its scholarly tastes and habits, its eager friendships and quick hatreds, its keen debates, its frank discussions of character and of deep political and religious questions, — all are safeguards against sloth, vulgarity, and depravity. Its society and not less its solitudes are full of teaching. Shams, conceit, and fictitious distinctions get no mercy. There is nothing but ridicule for bombast and sentimentality. Repression of genuine sentiment and emotion is indeed, in this College, carried too far. Reserve is more respectable than any undiscerning communicativeness. But neither Yankee shamefacedness nor English stolidity is admirable. This point especially touches you, young men, who are still undergraduates. When you feel a true admiration for a teacher, a glow of enthusiasm for work, a thrill of pleasure at some excellent saying, give it expression. Do not be ashamed of these emotions. Cherish the natural sentiment of personal devotion to the teacher who calls out your better powers. It is a great delight to serve an intellectual master. We Americans are but too apt to lose this happiness. German and French students get it. If ever in after years you come to smile at the youthful reverence you paid, believe me, it will be with tears in your eyes.

Many excellent persons see great offence in any system of college rank; but why should we expect more of young men than we do of their elders? How many men and women perform their daily tasks from the highest motives alone, — for the glory of God and the relief of man's estate? Most people work for bare bread, a few for cake. The college rank-list reinforces higher motives. In the campaign for character, no auxiliaries are to be refused. Next to despising the enemy, it is dangerous to reject allies. To devise a suitable method of estimating the fidelity and attainments of college students is, however, a problem which has long been under discussion, and has not yet received a satisfactory solution. The worst of rank as a stimulus is the self-reference it implies in the aspirants. The less a young man thinks about the cultivation of his mind, about his own mental progress, — about himself, in short, — the better.

The petty discipline of colleges attracts altogether too much attention both from friends and foes. It is to be remembered that the rules concerning decorum, however necessary to maintain the high standard of manners and conduct which characterizes this College, are nevertheless justly described as petty. What is technically called a quiet term cannot be accepted as the acme of University success. This success is not to be measured by the frequency or rarity of college punishments. The criteria of success or failure in a high place of learning are not the boyish escapades of an insignificant minority, nor the exceptional cases of ruinous vice. Each year must be judged by the added opportunities of instruction, by the prevailing enthusiasm in learning, and by the gathered wealth of culture and character. The best way to put boyishness to shame is to foster scholarship and manliness. The manners of a community cannot be improved by main force any more than its morals. The Statutes of the University need some amendment and reduction in the chapters on crimes and misdemeanors. But let us render to our fathers the justice we shall need from our sons. What is too minute or precise for our use was doubtless wise and proper in its day. It was to inculcate a reverent bearing and due consideration for things sacred that the regulations prescribed a black dress on Sunday. Black is not the only decorous wear in these days; but we must not seem, in ceasing from this particular mode of good manners, to think less of the gentle breeding of which only the outward signs, and not the substance, have been changed.

Harvard College has always attracted and still attracts students in all conditions of life. From the city trader or professional man, who may be careless how much his son spends at Cambridge, to the farmer or mechanic, who finds it a hard sacrifice to give his boy his time early enough to enable him to prepare for college, — all sorts and conditions of men have wished and still wish to send their sons hither. There are always scores of young men in this University who earn or borrow every dollar they spend here. Every year many young men enter this College without any resources whatever. If they prove themselves men of capacity and character, they never go away for lack of money. More than twenty thousand dollars a year is now devoted to aiding students of narrow means to compass their education, beside all the remitted fees and the numerous private benefactions. These latter are unfailing. Taken in connection with the proceeds of the funds applicable to the aid of poor students, they enable the Corporation to say that no good student need ever stay away from Cambridge, or leave college simply because he is poor. There is one uniform condition, however, on which help is given, — the recipient must be of promising ability and the best character. The community does not owe superior education to all children, but only to the *élite*, — to those who, having the capacity, prove by hard work that they have also the necessary perseverance and endurance. The process of preparing to enter college under the difficulties which poverty entails is just such a test of worthiness as is needed. At this moment there is no college in the country more eligible for a poor student than Harvard on the mere ground of economy. The scholarship funds are mainly the fruit of the last fifteen years. The future will take care of itself; for it is to be expected that the men who in this generation have had the benefit of these funds, and who succeed in after life, will pay many fold to their successors in need the debt which they owe, not to the College, but to benefactors whom they cannot even thank, save in heaven. No wonder that scholarships are founded. What greater privilege than this of giving young men of promise the coveted means of intellectual growth and freedom? The angels of heaven might envy mortals so fine a luxury. The happiness which the winning of a scholarship gives is not the recipient's alone: it flashes back to the home whence he came, and gladdens anxious hearts there. The good which it does is not his alone, but descends, multiplying at every step, through generations. Thanks to the beneficent mysteries of hereditary transmission, no capital earns such interest as personal culture. The poorest and the richest students are equally welcome here, provided that with their poverty or their wealth they bring capacity, ambition, and purity. The poverty of scholars is of inestimable worth in this money-getting nation. It maintains the true standards of virtue and honor. The poor friars, not the bishops, saved the Church. The poor scholars and preachers of duty defend the modern community against its own material prosperity. Luxury and learning are ill bed-fellows. Nevertheless, this College owes much of its distinctive character to those who bringing hither from refined homes good breeding, gentle tastes, and a manly delicacy, add to them openness and activity of mind, intellectual interests, and a sense of public duty. It is as high a privilege for a rich man's son as for a poor man's to resort to these academic halls, and so to take his proper place among cultivated and intellectual men. To lose altogether the presence of those who in early life have enjoyed the domestic and social advantages of wealth would be as great a blow to the College as to lose the sons of the poor. The interests of the College and the country are identical in this regard. The country suffers when the rich are ignorant and unrefined. Inherited wealth is an unmitigated curse when divorced from culture. Harvard College is sometimes reproached with being aristocratic. If by aristocracy be meant a stupid and pretentious caste, founded on wealth, and birth, and an affectation of European manners, no charge could be more preposterous: the College is intensely American in affection, and intensely democratic in temper. But there is an aristocracy to which the sons of Harvard have belonged, and let us hope will ever aspire to belong, — the aristocracy which excels in manly sports, carries off the honors and prizes of the learned professions, and bears itself with distinction in all fields of intellectual labor and combat; the aristocracy which in peace stands firmest for the public honor and renown, and in war rides first into the murderous thickets.

The attitude of the University in the prevailing discussions touching the education and fit employments of women demands brief explanation. America is the natural arena for these debates; for here the female sex has a better past and a better present than elsewhere. Americans, as a rule, hate disabilities of all sorts, whether religious, political, or social. Equality between the sexes, without privilege or oppression on either side, is the happy custom of American homes. While this great discussion is going on, it is the duty of the University to maintain a cautious and expectant policy. The Corporation will not receive women as students into the College proper, nor into any school whose discipline requires residence near the school. The difficulties involved in a common residence of hundreds of young men and women of immature character and marriageable age are very grave. The necessary police regulations are exceedingly burdensome. The Corporation are not influenced to this decision,

17

however, by any crude notions about the innate capacities of women. The world knows next to nothing about the natural mental capacities of the female sex. Only after generations of civil freedom and social equality will it be possible to obtain the data necessary for an adequate discussion of woman's natural tendencies, tastes, and capabilities. Again, the Corporation do not find it necessary to entertain a confident opinion upon the fitness or unfitness of women for professional pursuits. It is not the business of the University to decide this mooted point. In this country the University does not undertake to protect the community against incompetent lawyers, ministers, or doctors. The community must protect itself by refusing to employ such. Practical, not theoretical, considerations determine the policy of the University. Upon a matter concerning which prejudices are deep, and opinion inflammable, and experience scanty, only one course is prudent, or justifiable when such great interests are at stake, — that of cautious and well-considered experiment. The practical problem is to devise a safe, promising, and instructive experiment. Such an experiment the Corporation have meant to try in opening the newly established University Courses of Instruction to competent women. In these courses, the University offers to young women who have been to good schools, as many years as they wish of liberal culture in studies which have no direct professional value, to be sure, but which enrich and enlarge both intellect and character. The University hopes thus to contribute to the intellectual emancipation of women. It hopes to prepare some women better than they would otherwise have been prepared for the profession of teaching, the one learned profession to which women have already acquired a clear title. It hopes that the proffer of this higher instruction will have some reflex influence upon schools for girls, — to discourage superficiality, and to promote substantial education.

The governing bodies of the University are the Faculties, the Board of Overseers, and the Corporation. The University as a place of study and instruction is, at any moment, what the Faculties make it. The professors, lecturers, and tutors of the University are the living sources of learning and enthusiasm. They personally represent the possibilities of instruction. They are united in several distinct bodies, the academic and professional Faculties, each of which practically determines its own processes and rules. The discussion of methods of instruction is the principal business of these bodies. As a fact, progress comes mainly from the Faculties. This has been conspicuously the case with the Academic and Medical Faculties during the last fifteen or twenty years. The undergraduates used to have a notion that the time of the Academic Faculty was mainly devoted to petty discipline. Nothing could be farther from the truth. The Academic Faculty is the most active, vigilant, and devoted body connected with the University. It indeed is constantly obliged to discuss minute details, which might appear trivial to an inexperienced observer. But, in education, technical details tell. Whether German be studied by the Juniors once a week as an extra study, or twice a week as an elective, seems, perhaps, an unimportant matter; but, twenty years hence, it makes all the difference between a generation of Alumni who know German and a generation who do not. The Faculty renews its youth, through the frequent appointments of tutors and assistant professors, better and oftener than any other organization within the University. Two kinds of men make good teachers, — young men and men who never grow old. The incessant discussions of the Academic Faculty have borne much fruit: witness the transformation of the University since the beginning of President Walker's administration. And it never tires. New men take up the old debates, and one year's progress is not less than another's. The divisions within the Faculty are never between the old and the young officers. There are always old radicals and young conservatives.

The Medical Faculty affords another illustration of the same principle, — that for real University progress we must look principally to the teaching bodies. The Medical School to-day is almost three times as strong as it was fifteen years ago. Its teaching power is greatly increased, and its methods have been much improved. This gain is the work of the Faculty of the School.

If then the Faculties be so important, it is a vital question how the quality of these bodies can be maintained and improved. It is very hard to find competent professors for the University. Very few Americans of eminent ability are attracted to this profession. The pay has been too low, and there has been no gradual rise out of drudgery, such as may reasonably be expected in other learned callings. The law of supply and demand, or the commercial principle that the quality as well as the price of goods is best regulated by the natural contest between producers and consumers, never has worked well in the province of high education. And in spite of the high standing of some of its advocates, it is well-nigh certain that the so-called law never can work well in such a field. The reason is, that the demand for instructors of the highest class on the part of parents and trustees is an ignorant demand, and the supply of highly educated teachers is so limited that the consumer has not sufficient opportunities of informing himself concerning the real qualities of the article he seeks. Originally a bad judge, he remains a bad judge, because the supply is not sufficiently abundant and various to instruct him. Moreover, a need is not necessarily a demand. Everybody knows that the supposed law affords a very imperfect protection against short weight, adulteration, and sham, even in the case of those commodities which are most abundant in the market and most familiar to buyers. The most intelligent community is defenceless enough in buying clothes and groceries. When it comes to hiring learning, and inspiration and personal weight, the law of supply and demand breaks down altogether. A university cannot be managed like a railroad or a cotton mill.

There are, however, two practicable improvements in the position of college professors which will be of very good effect. Their regular stipend must and will be increased, and the repetitions which now harass them must be diminished in number. It is a strong point of the elective system, that by reducing the size of classes or divisions, and increasing the variety of subjects, it makes the professors' labors more agreeable.

Experience teaches that the strongest and most devoted professors will contribute something to the patrimony of knowledge; or if they invent little themselves, they will do something towards defending, interpreting, or diffusing the contributions of others. Nevertheless, the prime business of American professors in this generation must be regular and assiduous class teaching. With the exception of the endowments of the Observatory, the University does not hold a single fund primarily intended to secure to men of learning the leisure and means to prosecute original researches.

The organization and functions of the Board of Overseers deserve the serious attention of all men who are interested in the American method of providing the community with high education through the agency of private corporations. Since 1866 the Overseers have been elected by the Alumni. Five men are chosen each year to serve six years. The body has, therefore, a large and very intelligent constituency, and is rapidly renewed. The ingenious method of nominating to the electors twice as many candidates as there are places to be filled in any year is worthy of careful study as a device of possible application in politics. The real function of the Board of Overseers is to stimulate and watch the President and Fellows. Without the Overseers, the President and Fellows would be a board of private trustees, self-perpetuated and self-controlled. Provided as it is with two governing boards, the University enjoys that principal safeguard of all American governments, — the natural antagonism between two bodies of different constitution, powers, and privileges. While having with the Corporation a common interest of the deepest kind in the welfare of the University and the advancement of learning, the Overseers should always hold towards the Corporation an attitude of suspicious vigilance. They ought always to be pushing and prying. It would be hard to overstate the importance of the public supervision exercised by the Board of Overseers. Experience proves that our main hope for the permanence and ever-widening usefulness of the University must rest upon this double-headed organization. The English practice of setting up a single body of private trustees to carry on a school or charity according to the personal instructions of some founder or founders has certainly proved a lamentably bad one; and when we count by generations, the institutions thus established have proved short-lived. The same causes which have brought about the decline of English endowed schools would threaten the life of this University were it not for the existence of the Board of Overseers. These schools were generally managed by close corporations, self-elected, self-controlled, without motive for activity, and destitute of external stimulus and aid. Such bodies are too irresponsible for human nature. At the time of life at which men generally come to such places of trust, rest is sweet, and the easiest way is apt to seem the best way; and the responsibility of inaction, though really heavier, seems lighter than the responsibility of action. These corporations were often hampered by founders' wills and statutory provisions which could not be executed, and yet stood in the way of organic improvemenst. There was no systematic provision for thorough inspections and public reports thereupon. We cannot flatter ourselves that under like circumstances we should always be secure against like dangers. Provoked by crying abuses, some of the best friends of education in England have gone the length of maintaining that all these school endowments ought to be destroyed, and the future creation of such trusts rendered impossible. French law practically prohibits the creation of such trusts by private persons.

Incident to the Overseers' power of inspecting the University and publicly reporting upon its condition, is the important function of suggesting and urging improvements. The inertia of a massive University is formidable. A good past is positively dangerous, if it make us content with the present and so unprepared for the future. The present constitution of our Board of Overseers has already stimulated the Alumni of several other New-England colleges to demand a similar control over the property-holding board of Trustees which has heretofore been the single source of all authority.

We come now to the heart of the University, — the Corporation. This board holds the funds, makes appointments, fixes salaries, and has, by right, the initiative in all changes of the organic law of the University. Such an executive board must be small to be efficient. It must always contain men of sound judgment in finance; and literature and the learned professions should be adequately represented in it. The Corporation should also be but slowly renewed; for it is of the utmost consequence to the University that the Government should have a steady aim, and a prevailing spirit which is independent of individuals and transmissible from generation to generation. And what should this spirit be? First, it should be a catholic spirit. A University must be indigenous; it must be rich; but, above all, it must be free. The winnowing breeze of freedom must blow through all its chambers. It takes a hurricane to blow wheat away. An atmosphere of intellectual freedom is the native air of literature and science. This University aspires to serve the nation by training men to intellectual honesty and independence of mind. The Corporation demands of all its teachers that they be grave, reverent, and high-minded; but it leaves them, like their pupils, free. A University is built, not by a sect, but by a nation.

Secondly, the actuating spirit of the Corporation must be a spirit of fidelity, — fidelity to the many and various trusts reposed in them by the hundreds of persons who out of their penury or their abundance have given money to the President and Fellows of Harvard College in the beautiful hope of doing some perpetual good upon this earth. The Corporation has constantly done its utmost to make this hope a living fact. One hundred and ninety-nine years ago, William Pennoyer gave the rents of certain estates in the County of Norfolk, Eng., that "two fellows and two scholars for ever should be educated, brought up, and maintained" in this College. The income from this bequest has never failed; and to-day one of the four Pennoyer scholarships is held by a lineal descendant of William Pennoyer's brother Robert. So a lineal descendant of Governor Danforth takes this year the income of the property which Danforth bequeathed to the College in 1699. The Corporation have been as faithful in the greater things as in the less. They have been greatly blessed in one respect, — in the whole life of the Corporation, seven generations of men, nothing has ever been lost by malfeasance of officers or servants. A reputation for scrupulous fidelity to all trusts is the most precious possession of the Corporation. That safe, the College might lose every thing else and yet survive, — that lost beyond repair, and the days of the College would be numbered. Testators look first to the trustworthiness and permanence of the body which is to dispense their benefactions. The Corporation thankfully receive all gifts which may advance learning; but they believe that the interests of the University may be most effectually promoted by not restricting too narrowly the use to which a gift may be applied. Whenever the giver desires it, the Corporation will agree to keep any fund separately invested under the name of the giver, and to apply the whole proceeds of such investment to any object the giver may designate. By such special investment, however, the insurance which results from the absorption of a specific gift in the general funds is lost. A fund invested by itself may be impaired or lost by a single error of judgment in investing. The chance of such loss is small in any one generation, but appreciable in centuries. Such general designations as salaries, books, dormitories, public buildings, scholarships, graduate or undergraduate, scientific collections, and expenses of experimental laboratories, are of permanent significance and effect; while experience proves that too specific and minute directions concerning the application of funds must often fail of fulfilment, simply in consequence of the changing needs and habits of successive generations.

Again, the Corporation should always be filled with the spirit of enterprise. An institution like this College is getting decrepit when it sits down contentedly on its mortgages. On its invested funds the Corporation should be always seeking how safely to make a quarter of a per cent more. A quarter of one per cent means a new professorship. It should be always pushing after more professorships, better professors, more land and buildings, and better apparatus. It should be eager, sleepless, and untiring, never wasting a moment in counting laurels won, ever prompt to welcome and apply the liberality of the community, and liking no prospect so well as that of difficulties to be overcome and labors to be done in the cause of learning and public virtue.

You recognize, gentlemen, the picture which I have drawn in thus delineating the true spirit of the Corporation of this College. I have described the noble quintessence of the New-England character, — that character which has made us a free and enlightened people, — that character which, please God, shall yet do a great work in the world for the lifting up of humanity.

Apart from the responsibility which rests upon the Corporation, its actual labors are far heavier than the community imagines. The business of the University has greatly increased in volume and complexity during the past twenty years, and the draughts made upon the time and thought of every member of the Corporation are heavy indeed. The high honors of the function are in these days most generously earned.

The President of the University is primarily an executive officer; but, being a member of both governing boards and of all the Faculties, he has also the influence in their debates, to which his more or less perfect intimacy with the University and greater or less personal weight may happen to entitle him. An administrative officer who undertakes to do every thing himself, will do but little and that little ill. The President's first duty is that of supervision. He should know what each officer's and servant's work is, and how it is done. But the days are past in which the President could be called on to decide every thing from the purchase of a door-mat to the appointment of a professor. The principle of divided and subordinate responsibilities, which rules in government bureaus, in manufactories, and all great companies, which makes a modern army a possibility, must be applied in the University. The President should be able to discern the practical essence of complicated and long-drawn discussions. He must often pick out that promising part of theory which ought to be tested by experiment, and must decide how many of things desirable are also attainable, and what one of many projects is ripest for execution. He must watch and look before, — watch, to seize opportunities to get money, to secure eminent teachers and scholars, and to influence public opinion towards the advancement of learning, — and look before, to anticipate the due effect on the University of the fluctuations of public opinion on educational problems; of the progress of the institutions which feed the University; of the changing condition of the professions which the University supplies; of the rise of new professions; of the gradual alteration of social and religious habits in the community. The University must accommodate itself promptly to significant changes in the character of the people for whom it exists. The institutions of higher education in any nation are always a faithful mirror in which are sharply reflected the national history and character. In this mobile nation the action and reaction between the University and society at large are more sensitive and rapid than in stiffer communities. The President, therefore, must not need to see a house built before he can comprehend the plan of it. He can profit by a wide intercourse with all sorts of men, and by every real discussion on education, legislation, and sociology.

The most important function of the President is that of advising the Corporation concerning appointments, particularly about appointments of young men who have not had time and opportunity to approve themselves to the public. It is in discharging this duty that the President holds the future of the University in his hands. He cannot do it well unless he have insight, unless he be able to recognize, at times beneath some crusts, the real gentleman and the natural teacher. This is the one oppressive responsibility of the President: all other cares are light beside it. To see every day the evil fruit of a bad appointment must be the cruelest of official torments. Fortunately, the good effect of a judicious appointment is also inestimable; and here, as everywhere, good is more penetrating and diffusive than evil.

It is imperative that the Statutes which define the President's duties should be recast, and the customs of the College be somewhat modified, in order that lesser duties may not crowd out the greater. But, however important the functions of the President, it must not be forgotten that he is emphatically a constitutional executive. It is his character and his judgment which are of importance, not his opinions. He is the executive officer of deliberative bodies, in which decisions are reached after discussion by a majority vote. Those decisions bind him. He cannot force his own opinions upon anybody. A University is the last place in the world for a dictator. Learning is always republican. It has idols, but not masters.

What can the community do for the University? It can love, honor, and cherish it. Love it and honor it. The University is upheld by this public affection and respect. In the loyalty of her children she finds strength and courage. The Corporation, the Overseers, and the several Faculties need to feel that the leaders of public opinion, and especially the sons of the College, are at their back, always ready to give them a generous and intelligent support. Therefore we welcome the Chief Magistrate of the Commonwealth, the Senators, Judges, and other dignitaries of the State, who by their presence at this ancient ceremonial bear witness to the pride which Massachusetts feels in her eldest University. Therefore we rejoice in the presence of this throng of the Alumni, testifying their devotion to the College which, through all changes, is still their home. Cherish it. This University, though rich among American colleges, is very poor in comparison with the great universities of Europe. The wants of the American community have far outgrown the capacity of the University to supply them. We must try to satisfy the cravings of the select few as well as the needs of the average many. We cannot afford to neglect the Fine Arts. We need groves and meadows as well as barracks, and soon there will be no chance to get them in this expanding city. But, above all, we need professorships, books, and apparatus, that teaching and scholarship may abound.

And what will the University do for the community? First, it will make a rich return of learning, poetry, and piety. Secondly, it will foster the sense of public duty, — that great virtue which makes republics possible. The founding of Harvard College was an heroic act of public spirit. For more than a century the breath of life was kept in it by the public spirit of the Province and of its private benefactors. In the last fifty years the public spirit of the friends of the College has quadrupled its endowments. And how have the young men nurtured here in successive generations repaid the founders for their pious care? Have they honored freedom and loved their country? For answer we appeal to the records of the national service; to the lists of the senate, the cabinet, and the diplomatic service, and to the rolls of the army and navy. Honored men, here present, illustrate before the world the public quality of the graduates of this College. Theirs is no mercenary service. Other fields of labor attract them more and would reward them better; but they are filled with the noble ambition to deserve well of the republic. There have been doubts, in times yet recent, whether culture were not selfish; whether men of refined tastes and manners could really love Liberty, and be ready to endure hardness for her sake; whether, in short, gentlemen would in this century prove as loyal to noble ideas, as in other times they had been to kings. In yonder old playground, fit spot whereon to commemorate the manliness which there was nurtured, shall soon rise a noble monument which for generations will give convincing answer to such shallow doubts; for over its gates will be written, "In memory of the sons of Harvard who died for their country." The future of the University will not be unworthy of its past.

389-16